MW00450756

Design
David West
Children's Book Design
Illustrations
Wendie Harris
Tessa Barwick
Picture Research
Cecilia Weston-Baker
Editor
Denny Robson
Consultant
John Stidworthy

© Aladdin Books Ltd 1989
Designed and produced by
Aladdin Books Ltd
28 Percy Street
London W1P 9FF

*First Published in
Great Britain in 1988 by*
Franklin Watts
96 Leonard Street
London EC2A 4RH

First paperback edition published 1991

Hardback ISBN 0 86313 763 6
Paperback ISBN 0 07496 0669 X

Printed in Belgium

This book tells you all about the different
types of crocodiles and alligators – where
they live, what they eat and how they survive.
Find out some surprising facts about them in
the boxes on each page. The identification
chart at the back of the book will help you
when you see crocodiles and alligators in
zoos or in the wild.

The little square shows
you the size of the
animal. Each side
represents 2m (6½ft).

A red square means
that the animal is in
need of protection. See
the survival file.

The picture opposite shows a young crocodile hatching from its egg

FIRST SIGHT
CROCODILES AND ALLIGATORS

Lionel Bender

GLOUCESTER PRESS
London · New York · Toronto · Sydney

Introduction

Crocodiles and alligators are the only survivors of a group of reptiles that dominated the Earth about 200 to 65 million years ago, a group which included the dinosaurs. The crocodile and alligator family consists of 22 species of reptiles that are adapted for life in and around water. The family includes the true crocodiles, which live in Africa, Asia and Australia, the alligators of North and South America and China, the caimans of South America, and the Gharial, or Gavial, of India. Together they are known as crocodilians.

Crocodiles and alligators are most common in hot tropical regions, but they also live in areas where there are warm summers and cool winters. They are all hunters and they feed on animals that range from deer and cattle to fish and birds.

Contents

Cold-blooded **7**
Life in water **8**
Out on land **11**
Big and small **12**
Teeth and jaws **15**
Hunting and feeding **16**
Attack and defence **18**
Senses and sounds **21**
Courtship and mating **22**
Eggs and hatchlings **24**
Growing up **26**
Survival file **28**
Identification chart **30**
Make Crocodilian Snap **30**
Index **32**

◁ **An American Alligator stretches out of the water to catch a young Egret**

◁ **A crocodile basks in the sun on a riverbank**

midday

Most crocodiles keep their bodies at 30-35°C (85-97°F). This is a few degrees cooler than ours. They become sluggish at below 20°C (68°F).

morning

evening

When the sun gets too hot, the crocodile slinks into the water.

A crocodile warms up by basking in the morning sun.

It warms up again in late afternoon and early evening.

Cold-blooded

Crocodiles and alligators, like other reptiles, are cold-blooded. This means they cannot adjust their body temperature by producing body heat, as we can. They have to rely on their surroundings to keep their bodies warm enough to work properly. This is why they are most common in warm countries.

When they are active, or as they bask in the sun, their temperature rises. Crocodiles and alligators usually lie with their mouths open when they are too hot. This helps them lose heat. They cannot sweat to cool down. But when their temperature increases well above normal, they must stop moving, rest in the shade, or slink into the water.

7

Life in water

Crocodilians are difficult to see when they lie in the water. They are often mistaken for logs. Their eyes and nostrils are set high on their heads. This means that they can see and breathe when they are floating almost totally underwater. They use sideways sweeps of their large, powerful, flattened tails to swim along. When danger threatens, they sink quickly downwards and backwards using a sudden upward movement of their webbed hind feet.

Underwater, crocodilians keep their nostrils and ears closed. A special flap of skin sweeps sideways across each eye to give protection during diving. The animals can hold their breath for more than an hour.

A Gharial swimming in a river, showing the sideways motion of its tail

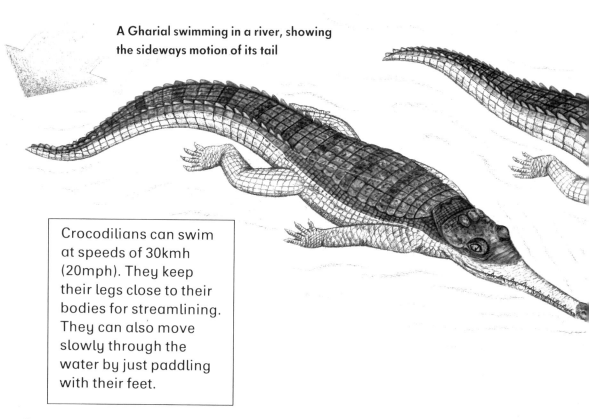

Crocodilians can swim at speeds of 30kmh (20mph). They keep their legs close to their bodies for streamlining. They can also move slowly through the water by just paddling with their feet.

An American Alligator cruises through the water

The crocodilian's shoulder and hip girdles connect the massive leg bones to the backbone. The front legs have five toes, the back legs four.

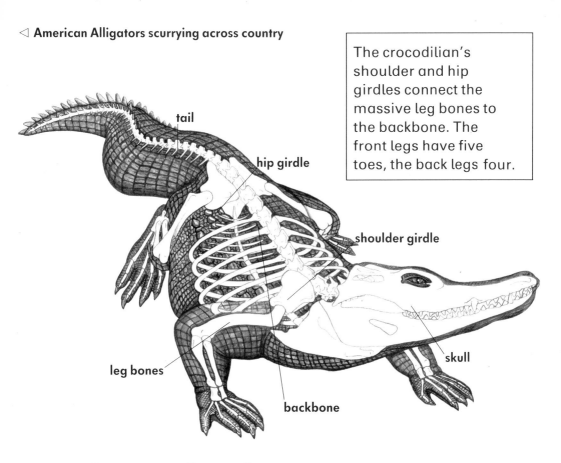

tail

hip girdle

shoulder girdle

leg bones

skull

backbone

Out on land

The Australian Freshwater Crocodile and the Nile Crocodile can gallop across country, with front and back legs working together like a bounding squirrel. But usually crocodiles walk on dry land by stretching their legs and lifting their bodies well off the ground. Alligators and caimans usually slink about, moving slowly forward on their stomachs with their legs spread out either side.

The Gharial and the Saltwater Crocodile of South-east Asia rarely move more than a few metres from their river and estuary homes. But species that live in ponds and lakes, such as the Indian Marsh Crocodile, may travel many kilometres overland in search of water if their homes dry up.

Big and small

Crocodiles and alligators grow rapidly in areas where they can find plenty of food and it is warm all year round. The biggest crocodilian on record was an Estuarine Crocodile from Bengal that is thought to have measured 10m (33ft) in length and weighed more than two tonnes. The Smooth-fronted Caiman and African Dwarf Crocodile, on the other hand, barely reach 1.5m (5ft) as adults.

Crocodilians continue to grow throughout their lives and they can live for many years – American Alligators may live for up to 70 years. This means that several species can grow very large. But today poachers kill the largest specimens and so individuals over 6m (20ft) long are rare.

A Dwarf Caiman looks for a meal with only its head out of the water

The Estuarine Crocodile, like all crocodilians, continues to grow throughout its life ▷

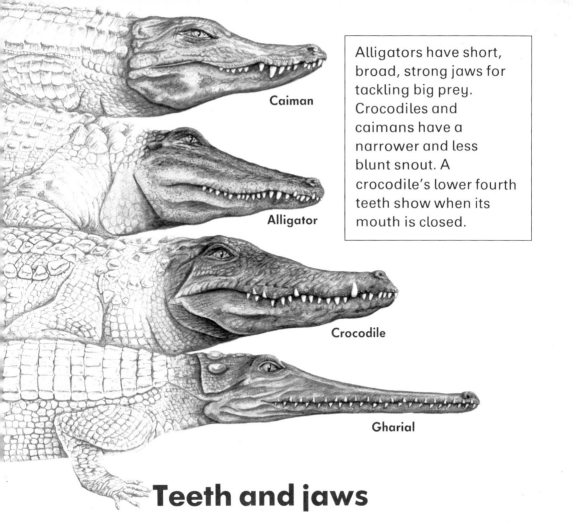

Caiman

Alligator

Crocodile

Gharial

Alligators have short, broad, strong jaws for tackling big prey. Crocodiles and caimans have a narrower and less blunt snout. A crocodile's lower fourth teeth show when its mouth is closed.

Teeth and jaws

The Gharial is a fish-eater which has about 160 teeth. These are small and pointed so that the animal can keep hold of its slippery prey. Crocodiles and alligators have about 100 teeth. Their teeth are good for holding flesh, but not for cutting or chewing it. Crocodiles hold food in their teeth and thrash it about to tear it apart. They can then swallow the food in large chunks.

Crocodiles and alligators often lose teeth in struggles with large prey. But the teeth are quickly replaced. Each tooth contains a small replacement tooth inside it. A crocodilian may produce fifty or more sets of teeth within its lifetime.

◁ **A Gharial with its bulb-like nose**

Hunting and feeding

Fish, birds, snakes, lizards, frogs, turtles, rats, deer, zebra and cattle are all part of the diet of crocodiles, alligators and caimans. As babies, however, crocodilians eat mainly insects, frogs and small fish. The Gharial eats nothing but fish.

The American Alligator often captures prey by lying in wait in shallow water or within pools along the river bank. As a victim approaches, the alligator seizes it, drags it underwater and then tears it apart. Crocodiles sometimes attack and eat one another. They will even eat people. But this only happens when they cannot find their normal prey. Crocodilians also feed on dead animals – they are both scavengers and hunters.

A young crocodile grips a fish in its pointed teeth

A Nile Crocodile eats a zebra killed by another hunter ▷

Attack and defence

A crocodilian's most effective weapons are its powerful jaws. Once these are closed tight, no animal can escape their grip. A crocodilian will sometimes use its tail to knock over an animal before trying to eat it. Male alligators fight over females at mating time, tearing at each other with their teeth.

Despite their fierceness, crocodiles and alligators do have enemies. Crocodiles may be killed in fights with lions and leopards. A mother elephant or hippo will also attack a crocodile that threatens her young. But most crocodilians are so well camouflaged in drab greens and browns that they usually surprise and then easily overpower their prey.

Male alligators will often attack one another fiercely

An American Alligator, covered with and surrounded by algae, waits for a meal ▷

Senses and sounds

Vision and hearing are crocodilians' most important senses. They rely mainly on vision to hunt and capture prey. When their ears are out of the water, they can hear well too. They keep in touch with one another using a variety of sounds. Baby crocodiles peep loudly when they hatch from their eggs so that their mother will help them out of the nest. Male and female crocodilians roar and croak loudly at each other at mating time.

Crocodiles and alligators swallow their food underwater in large chunks and so they do not need good senses of smell and taste. Their skin is thick and leathery and not very sensitive to touch.

Crocodiles and alligators possess a third eyelid that moves sideways across the eye.

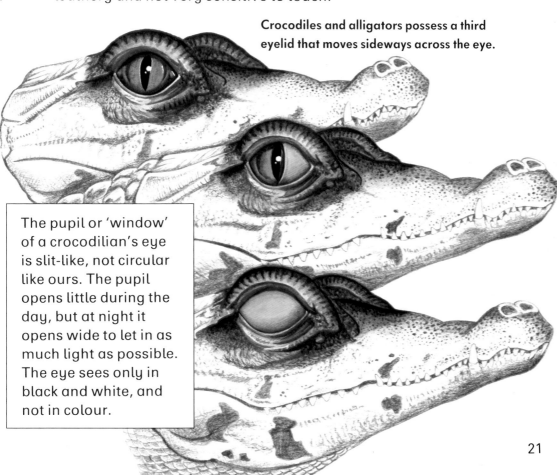

The pupil or 'window' of a crocodilian's eye is slit-like, not circular like ours. The pupil opens little during the day, but at night it opens wide to let in as much light as possible. The eye sees only in black and white, and not in colour.

21

Courtship and mating

At mating time, the male crocodilian courts the female. An adult male Gharial has a swelling on its snout that probably helps to attract a mate. A male Nile Crocodile displays his desire to mate by thrashing about in the water and keeping his mouth open. He comes alongside the female in the water and puts his legs on her back. The pair then sink to the bottom of the river or lake and mate.

About two months after mating, the female is ready to lay her eggs. While she is pregnant she prepares a nest, which acts as an incubator to protect the eggs and keep them warm. The male rarely helps in nest building, or in looking after the eggs.

A male Gharial (left) approaches a female as a plover looks on

A female Estuarine Crocodile guards her nest ▷

An alligator's egg showing the developing embryo within the fluid-filled sac

The shell of a crocodile or alligator's egg is hard and fragile, like a bird's egg. Inside the egg, yolk provides the embryo with food. A sac which is filled with fluid surrounds the embryo and protects it from damage.

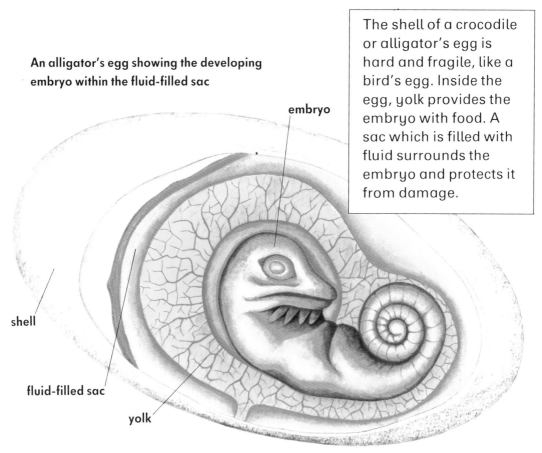

embryo

shell

fluid-filled sac

yolk

Eggs and hatchlings

A female alligator or female Gharial lays between 15 and 80 eggs. A female Nile Crocodile lays as many as 90, each the size of a goose egg. The Gharial digs out a hollow in the ground for a nest. Alligators make a heap of water plants, lay the eggs on the top, then cover them with more plant material. Crocodiles often just bury their eggs in the sand.

The baby crocodilians hatch between nine and 17 weeks later. Sometimes the mother picks up eggs that have not hatched and gently crushes them in her jaws to free the young. Hatchlings look like small versions of their parents. Even those of the 6m (20ft) long Nile Crocodile are less than 30cm (12in) in length.

Young crocodilians often hatch within moments of each other ▷

Growing up

Newborn crocodiles and alligators cannot look after themselves very well. Many are eaten by fish, birds, mammals and other reptiles, especially large lizards such as monitors. However, their mothers usually protect them for the first few months. Nile and Estuarine Crocodile mothers often carry their young from the nest to the water in their mouths. A mother Gharial will carry her young on her back.

The young grow quickly, almost doubling their length in the first year. The American Alligator grows 25 to 30cm (10 to 12in) each year. It is adult when it is five years old. Most crocodilians are ready to mate by the time they are eight years old.

A young alligator hitches a ride on its mother's back

A young crocodile about to devour a crab ▷

Survival file

In many parts of Africa, South America, Australia and India, the native people kill alligators and crocodiles for food. This hunting has been going on for hundreds of years. But because these people only kill as many animals as they need, they do not threaten the survival of crocodilians. Since the 1950s, however, commercial hunters have killed crocodilians in their tens of thousands just for their skins. The skins are used to make handbags, shoes and wallets which are sold in shops all over the world.

In a nature reserve, crocodiles are given water buffalo to eat

Crocodiles and alligators are now also threatened by local farmers, who destroy their homes. The farmers drain lakes, ponds and swamps for land on which to graze their animals or grow crops. In India, hunting and habitat destruction reduced the number of Gharials in the wild to less than 100 in 1974.

Since about 1975, there has been a worldwide ban on trade in the skins of most crocodiles and alligators. But illegal hunting and egg-collecting still go on. There is also a growing trade in capturing crocodilians to be shown in wildlife parks and kept as pets. Most of those sold as pets are killed once they get too big.

Trade in crocodilian skins continues

Rangers sometimes have to kill alligators

In India, Australia and America, there are now crocodile and alligator farms that are helping to increase the numbers of crocodilians in the wild. Eggs are taken from the wild and kept safely in incubators. The hatchlings are looked after and fed until they are big and strong enough to be released back into the wild. The young are taken to rivers and lakes around the world.

Identification chart

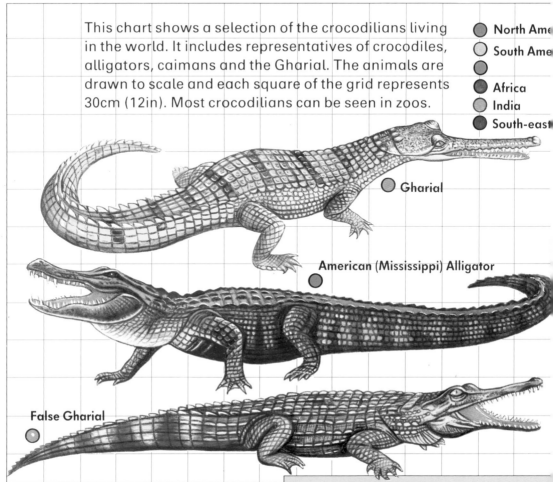

This chart shows a selection of the crocodilians living in the world. It includes representatives of crocodiles, alligators, caimans and the Gharial. The animals are drawn to scale and each square of the grid represents 30cm (12in). Most crocodilians can be seen in zoos.

- North Ame
- South Ame
-
- Africa
- India
- South-east

Gharial

American (Mississippi) Alligator

False Gharial

Make Crocodilian Snap

1. Trace the heads of the four types of crocodilian shown on these pages onto pieces of cardboard.

2. Make about six of each type of playing card.

3. Use the cards to play Snap or Pairs, matching the shapes of the heads and tooth patterns.

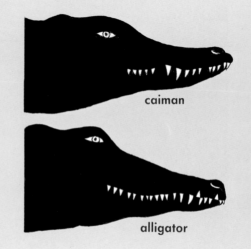

caiman

alligator

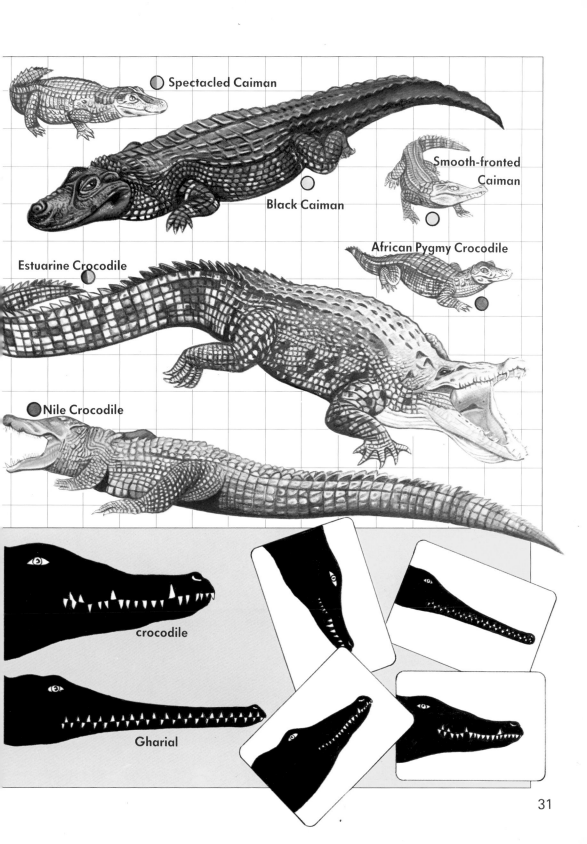

Spectacled Caiman

Black Caiman

Smooth-fronted Caiman

African Pygmy Crocodile

Estuarine Crocodile

Nile Crocodile

crocodile

Gharial

Index

A   age 12, 26
Alligator 5, 11, 15,
21, 24, 30, 31
American 9, 10,
12, 17, 18, 30

B   babies 16, 21, 24
basking 7
bones 11
breathing 8

C   Caiman 5, 11, 15, 17
Black 31
Smooth-fronted
12, 31
Spectacled 31
camouflage 18
cold-blooded 7
Courtship 22
Crocodile (true) 5,
15, 21, 30, 31
African dwarf 12
African pygmy 31
Australian
Freshwater 11
Estuarine 12, 22,
26, 31
Indian Marsh 11

Nile 11, 16, 22, 24,
26, 31
Saltwater 11

D   diving 8
distribution 5, 30, 31

E   ears 8, 21
eggs 21, 22, 24, 29
enemies 18, 26
eyes 8, 21

F   False Gharial 30
feeding and food 12,
15, 16, 21, 24
feet 8

G   Gharial 5, 8, 9, 11,
15, 17, 22, 24, 26,
29, 30
growth 12, 26

H   hearing 21
heat, coping with 7
hunting 16, 21

J   jaws 15, 18

K   killing of 28, 29

L   land, life on 11
legs 8, 11

M   mating 18, 21

N   nest 22
nostrils and nose 8,
15

S   senses 21
size 12, 26, 30, 31
skin 21, 28
skull 11
sounds 21
survival 28-29
swimming 8

T   tail 8, 11, 18
teeth 15, 16
temperature, body 7
toes 11

W   walking 11
water, life in 8, 9, 11,
16, 22
weapons 18

Photographic Credits:
Cover, title page and
pages 4, 6, 9, 12, 13, 18,
19, 23, 25 and 29 (top):
Bruce Coleman; pages
10, 14, 22 and 26:
Ardea; pages 16 and
27: Frank Lane
Agency; pages 17, 20
and 28: Planet Earth;
page 29 (bottom):
Frank Spooner Agency.

PRINTED IN BELGIUM BY
proost
INTERNATIONAL BOOK PRODUCTION